Love to Sew and Sew with Love...

A Bustle & Sew Publication

ISBN-13: 978-1490333458

ISBN-10: 1490333452

First published 2013 by:
Bustle & Sew
Coombe Leigh
Chillington
Kingsbridge
Devon TQ7 2LE
UK

www.bustleandsew.com

For my daughter Rosie, with love xxx

The Bustle & Sew Magazine is simply the nicest (and best value) way to build your collection of Bustle & Sew patterns. Try your first issue for just $1 and receive your free gift "The Stitcher's Companion" too.

Visit the Bustle & Sew website to learn more.

www.bustleandsew.com

Contents

Here I sit and wait like this
Until I get my Christmas kiss.

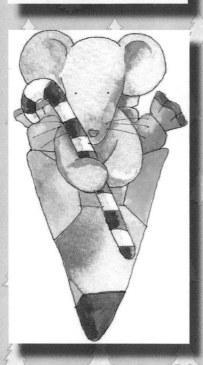

Introduction

Christmas is a wonderful time of year - a time for gifts and giving, family and friends, feasting and fun - as we celebrate the birth of the baby Jesus so far away and long ago.

It's so enjoyable to create for Christmas-time - whether you want to decorate your own home, or you're planning presents and surprises for your nearest and dearest. And if you're looking for ideas that are just that little bit special - but don't cost the earth or take hours to create, then you're sure to find just what you're looking for in this little book. I've collected together my favourite Bustle & Sew Christmas designs from the last three years - so you'll discover Angel Pigs, Baby Owls, Reindeer and even a giraffe!

There's a mixture of sewing, embroidery, softie-making and applique within these pages, and none of the designs are too difficult. They should all be easily within reach of a moderately experienced sewer, while many are suitable for beginners too. All have been previously published within the Bustle & Sew Magazine, but are collected together all in one place for the very first time. I've checked, reviewed and tweaked them so you can be confident of achieving the very best results - every single time!

Finally, I hope that wherever you are, and whatever you have planned this Christmas, that you will have a wonderful festive season.

Helen xx

Advent

For Christians, the weeks preceding Christmas Day itself are collectively known as Advent - celebrating the coming of Christ. Advent begins on the fourth Sunday before Christmas Day, which is known as Advent Sunday and can fall on any of the last four days of November or the first three days of December.

Excited children love to use Advent Calendars to count off the days until Christmas Day, and I have three here for you to choose from - Santa and his Reindeer, some enchanting baby owls and a Nativity scene featuring the Holy Family in the stable at Bethlehem.

These days mass-produced calendars are very inexpensive - even when they are filled with chocolate, but they are also rather impersonal and when discarded form part of our ever-growing litter problem. I think it's so much nicer to give a homemade calendar, made with love that will become a family heirloom - brought out and enjoyed year after year, forming part of your own family's Christmas traditions.

Baby Owls Advent Calendar

These baby owls have all hung up their Christmas stockings in the hope that Santa will remember them this Christmas Eve.

Deceptively easy project featuring freestyle machine embroidery - the stockings are stitched and then cut out. Then simply peg them to the calendar with those miniature clothes pegs you use for hanging cards.

Finished calendar measures 19" x 26".

You will need:

- 19 x 26 ¼" piece of medium weight navy blue fabric

- 19 x 26" piece of light-weight batting

- 19 x 7 ¼" piece of medium weight brown check fabric

- 20" x 6" piece of brown felt for tree (if you have a shorter, fatter piece this is fine, you can join it in the middle and stitch over the join).

- 1 FQ red polka dot fabric for stockings .

- 24" square red felt for backing stockings .

- 12" x 6" cream/blue polka dot fabric for stocking tops .

- Assorted scraps of fabric in browns, creams and other natural colours for the owls' bodies .

- Assorted scraps of fabric in greens for leaves .

- 5" square gold fabric for star

- 6" square of beige felt for eyes

- 4" square aqua blue fabric for eyes

- Small amount yellow felt for beaks and matching floss for stitching feet.

- 7 pairs of ¼" buttons for eyes

- 2 ½ yards baker's twine, and a needle it will fit through

- 3 yards bias binding

- 1" curtain rings for hanging

- 24 (or 25 if preferred) small pegs - the sort you can purchase for hanging cards.

- 8" square white cotton fabric suitable for printing numbers on. (Either use your printer, or write with a fabric marker, or use a stamp to mark the numbers. If you're using a printer, then I have provided the numbers I used later in the pattern.) .

- Darning/embroidery foot for your sewing machine.

- Black, cream and navy thread for your needle

- Bondaweb or fabric adhesive

- Temporary fabric marker pen

9

Background and Tree:

- Join your navy and blue fabrics along one 19" edge using a ¼" seam allowance. Press seam open.

- Trace tree shapes onto Bondaweb using the template on the next page. You will need to resize this template - the tree measures 19" tall from top to bottom, or simply cut the shapes freehand using the template image as a guide. Do not cut straight lines - the tree limbs should be gently curving and organic with rounded ends.

- Position your tree on the background, centering it horizontally. The base of the trunk should be 1 ½" up from the bottom of the background panel.

- Underlap the branches with the trunk as shown by the dotted lines on the template so there are no gaps.

- When you're happy with the positioning iron into place.

- With black thread in your machine needle and a lighter colour in your bobbin (this will give a less harsh effect) stitch twice around the edges of the tree trunk and branches. You are aiming for a scribbled effect - don't be too neat. If you like, you could also include a few knots and twirls as you stitch as shown in the image.

- Now trace onto Bondaweb, fuse to your green fabrics, and cut out 24 simple leaf shapes (see photograph for guidance).

- Position these leaves at the end of the branches, again using the photograph as guidance for positioning (there is no right and wrong!).

- When you're happy with the positioning iron into place, then machine stitch as shown below, going twice around the edge and then up into the middle and back to look like the centre vein of the leaf.

- Press lightly on the back then place to one side for the time being.

Make your owls:

- Using the template, trace the shapes onto Bondaweb. You may need to re-size the template - each owl should measure 3" tall.

- Then cut 7 owl bodies from your brown fabrics, 7 chests from cream, 7 beige felt spectacles and 14 aqua eyes.

- Position owls on branches using the photograph at the beginning of this pattern as a guide. Start with the bodies, then chests, spectacles

Tree template. Cut branches separately and overlap with trunk as shown by dotted lines. Tree measures 19" from bottom of trunk to its tip.

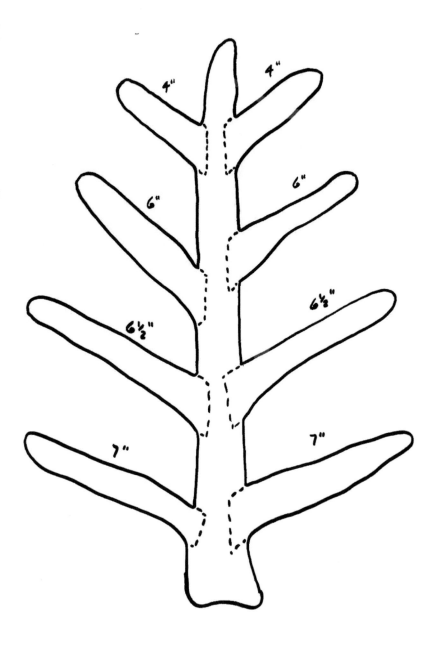

11

and eyes. The spectacles overlap the chests as shown by the dotted line on the template.

- When you're happy with the positioning of your owls fuse them into place by ironing.

- Add small triangles of yellow felt for beaks, then machine stitch your owls to the background panel.

- Stitch buttons to eyes with black floss, and indicate feet with a few straight stitches in yellow floss.

Owl measures 3" high

Make your stockings:

- Make a sandwich from red felt, Bondaweb and red polka dot fabric, ironing them together.

- Then draw around your stocking template 24 or 25 times using your temporary fabric marker pen

- Your stocking template should measure 2" high. Reverse some of the stockings so they will hang in opposite directions.

- .Print onto fabric and cut out the numbers for your stockings (or cut circles of white fabric and stamp or write the numbers on to them). Fuse numbers to stockings.

- Fuse Bondaweb onto the reverse of your cream and blue dotty fabric, then trace and cut out 24 or 25 stocking tops.

- Fuse stocking tops to stockings.

- With your darning foot and black thread in your needle machine stitch twice around edge of stocking just inside the lines you drew around the template. Make a few extra lines to indicate toe and heel of stocking and go around cream and blue dotty stocking top twice as well. Go around the numbers once. It's much easier to stitch such small pieces before you cut them out!

- Cut your stockings out. If any of the lines you drew can be seen then remove them with water or wait for them to fade (depending on the type of marker pen you used).

- Press lightly on reverse.

- Place to one side for the moment.

Assemble your calendar:

- Make a sandwich from your backing fabric (right side down), batting and calendar front (right side up) and pin or tack together.

- With navy thread in your needle and your darning foot, quilt around the edge of the tree, leaves and owl, changing the thread in your needle to brown when you quilt around the base of the tree.

- Bind the edges of your calendar with your bias binding.

- Now you're going to add your baker's twine to the branches to hang the stockings.

- Cut a 15" length of twine and thread it into your needle and push it through the front of your quilted calendar right to the back, leaving most of it at the front.

- Unthread your needle and make a knot in the twine.

- Thread your needle again and push through at the other end of the branch again securing with a knot at the back.

- Repeat for all the branches.

- Trim the tails of twine as shown in the image.

- Stitch the two curtain rings to the back for hanging (or you could use a quilt hanger if preferred,)

- Peg your stockings to the twine with the miniature pegs - one each day until Christmas!

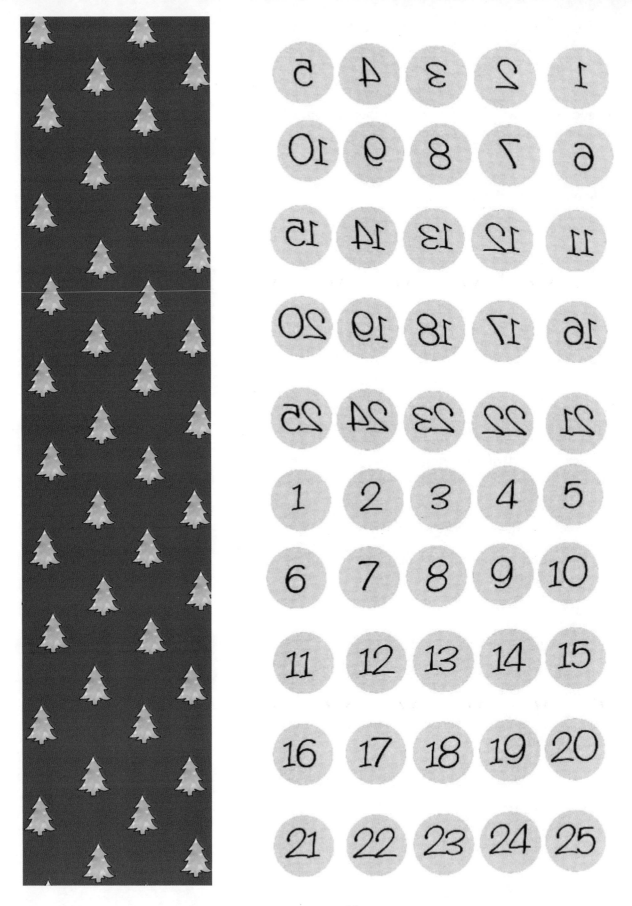

Nativity Advent Calendar

Count down to Christmas with this machine-applique Advent calendar. A really fun project – and a great chance to use up all those scraps to create something totally unique.

I have mounted my calendar on an artist's canvas block, but you could use a piece of MDF or frame yours (without glass) instead.

If you are able to use your computer and printer to print on fabric that's great and I've supplied numbers 1 – 24 for you to use. They're the same as for the Baby Owls Advent Calendar and you'll find them on page 14. If you can't do this, then you could always stamp, write with fabric marker or embroider the numbers instead. The little discs with the dates are applied to the background using Velcro dots – the sort offices use for noticeboard displays. They are self-adhesive and are easily obtained from any good stationer.

You will need:

- Artist's canvas block A3 size (that's 297 x 420 mm or 11.7" x 16.5")

- Piece of red gingham fabric measuring A3 size plus the depth of your block plus 1" all the way round.

- 16" x 10 ½" piece of white fabric (406 x 267 mm)

- 11 ½" x 9" piece of natural coloured fabric (292 x 229 mm)

- 56" (1m 42cm) red ric-rac braid

- 4" square piece of blue felt for Mary's robe

- 4" square piece of brown felt/fabric for Joseph's robe

- 6 x 4" piece of straw coloured felt/fabric for thatched roof of stable

- 2" square piece of white felt for dove

- Assorted scraps of fabric for rest of the design.

- Black, neutral and red thread for sewing machine needle

- Neutral thread for bobbin

- Embroidery floss in dark brown, dusky pink, yellow, gold and silver

- Tapestry or 4-ply wool for straw in 2 shades of brown or yellow

- Button for star (optional, you can embroider star if you prefer)

- Note: All fabrics used must be non-stretchy

For date numbers:

- Suitable white fabric to transfer numbers onto – usually white cotton – measuring 12" (300 mm) square

- 12" (300 mm) square piece of heavy duty interfacing

- 12" (300 mm) square piece of white or natural coloured felt

- 24 self-adhesive Velcro dots or squares (less than 1" square or trim to fit)

- Spray fabric adhesive

- Staple gun to attach fabric to artist's block or board

- Temporary (eg light fade or washable) fabric marker

Make your applique picture:

- Fold your piece of natural fabric into four quarters and press lightly with your hand to find the centre point. Transfer the design at the end of this pattern to your natural fabric using whichever method you prefer. This transferred design will act as a guide to help you position your applique shapes.

Before you begin, there are a few basic rules:

- Always begin at the "back" of the picture and work forwards (eg start with Mary's halo and finish with her robe (see illustration on following page)

- Always cut an "underlap" so you don't have two cut edges butted up against each other - the bottom piece should extend a little way beyond the edge of the piece above.

- Use the largest scissors you feel comfortable with to cut your shapes (I always use dressmaker's shears) and cut your shape in long smooth motions. This will give you a much nicer, smoother edge.

- Use black or a dark thread in your machine needle, but a much lighter thread in the bobbin. This breaks up the line - using the same colour in both appears much heavier.

- Go around the edges twice, but don't try to follow exactly the same line, you are aiming for a sort of "scribble" effect.

- You may find it easier to reduce the pressure on your presser foot - or possibly machine with a darning foot or freehand - whichever you prefer.

- Wherever possible, I prefer to use spray fabric adhesive for applique as it's easier to peel off and reposition than Bondaweb if things are going a bit wonky. But again, that's personal preference.

- On the next page you'll find detailed guidance for Mary, then work Joseph and Jesus in the same way.

- The stable and dove are easy, just simple shapes with almost no overlap. Cut out your shapes with an underlap allowance for lower pieces. I

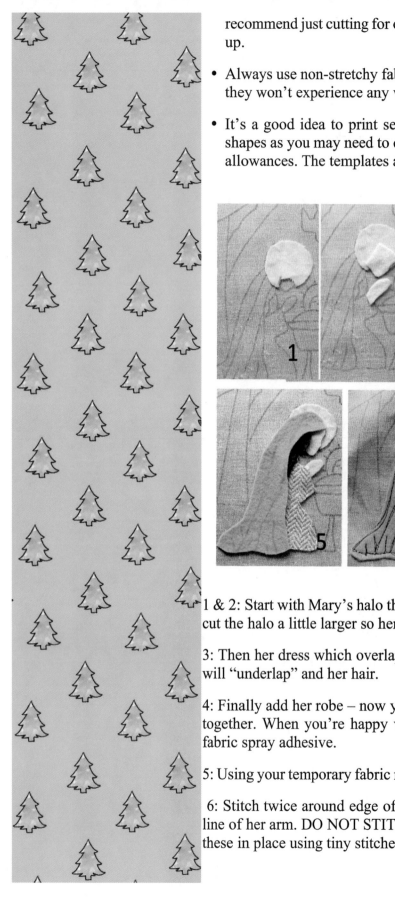

recommend just cutting for one element at a time to avoid getting mixed up.

- Always use non-stretchy fabric and don't worry about finishing edges, they won't experience any wear so any fraying will be minimal.

- It's a good idea to print several copies of the picture for cutting out shapes as you may need to cut into other pieces when cutting underlap allowances. The templates are actual size.

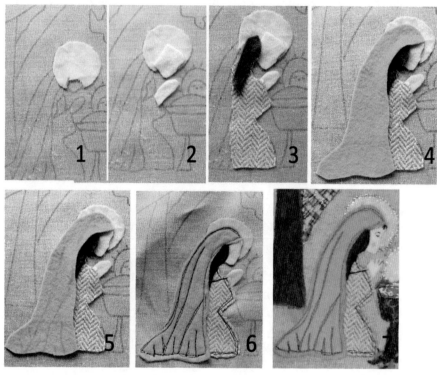

1 & 2: Start with Mary's halo then add her face and hand. Notice how I've cut the halo a little larger so her face sits partly on top of it.

3: Then her dress which overlaps her wrist – again cut a little longer so it will "underlap" and her hair.

4: Finally add her robe – now you can see how the design begins to come together. When you're happy with the positioning, secure in place with fabric spray adhesive.

5: Using your temporary fabric marker, mark the fold lines on Mary's robe.

6: Stitch twice around edge of robe, dress and hair. Stitch fold lines and line of her arm. DO NOT STITCH around her face, hands or halo. Secure these in place using tiny stitches in neutral coloured thread.

- Work Joseph, Jesus and the manger in the same way as Mary.

- Now take two strands of gold embroidery floss and work around the edge of Mary and Joseph's halos in stem stitch.

- Work around Jesus' halo in blanket stitch as shown.

- Work eyes in a single strand of dark brown floss and Mary's fringe in 2 strands of dark brown floss all in straight stitch.

- Mark fingers on hands in a single strand of dark brown floss.

- Work a couple of small straight stitches in dusky pink for rosy cheeks.

- Work criss-cross stitches in wool for straw.

- Apply stable pieces and machine around edges.

- Work zig-zags at the end to represent ends of thatch/pillars.

- Apply dove and secure to background fabric with small straight stitches.

- Work eye in dark brown and beak in yellow floss.

- Stem stitch around edge of dove in two strands of silver floss.

- Attach button for star (or embroider star) and work some long stitches in 2 strands of gold floss to represent rays.

- Blot to remove marker lines if necessary, then press on reverse.

- Turn under ½" (1 cm) seam allowance all the way around, press and stitch with natural coloured thread in needle.

Assemble panel:

- Take your rectangle of white fabric and turn under ½" (1 cm) seam allowance all the way around, press.

- Centre on red gingham fabric and pin or tack in place, then machine to background fabric.

- Apply red ric-rac braid all around the edge with red thread in machine needle. Press on reverse.

- Centre on artist's block. Fold excess fabric to back and attach to block at the back with staple gun. Work from the centre of each side outwards and keep your fabric taut but not stretched. Mitre the corners.

- Apply the white part of your velro dots to the white fabric borders, spacing them evenly. When you're happy with the positioning press down firmly to make sure they're securely attached.

Make date numbers:

- Print numbers on page 14 onto 12" square of fabric. (or embroider/stamp numbers if preferred)

- Make a sandwich of your printed numbers, heavy duty interfacing and backing felt. Join together using fabric adhesive.

- Cut out discs and secure the three layers together around the edges with machine zig-zag stitch.

- Apply one square/dot of Velcro to the back of each disc. Now they're ready to apply to your calendar throughout December - and you're done!!

Night Before Christmas Advent Calendar

And not just the night before Christmas but every night in December with this 25-pocket Advent Calendar featuring Santa and his reindeer (can you spot Rudolph). Nice roomy pockets for those all-important treats – will make a lovely decorative addition to your home in the run-up to Christmas.

Finished calendar measures 36" x 20" (approx)

You will need:

- 15 x 8" cream linen or other fabric suitable for embroidery

- 48" cotton lace for border of embroidery picture

- 25 x 5" squares quilting weight fabric to make pockets (I used a Moda charm pack in Glace) 1

- 0 x 8" piece white cotton for printing numbers on to Transfer paper suitable for your printer (if you don't want to print and transfer the numbers then you could stitch or stamp them onto suitable fabric)

- 36 x 20" linen or other suitable fabric for base

- 36 x 20" panel medium weight canvas for stiffening (or you could use heavy-weight interfacing)

- 3 ½ yards ½" bias binding

- 2 brass curtain rings

- Non-permanent fabric marker

- DMC stranded floss in colours: 224, 347, 826, 839, 840, 842, 906, 986, 3811, BLANC, E168, E3821, E436

Embroidery:

You will need to resize the transfer on the next page. Your finished embroidery should measure 13" wide x 6" tall. It is worked in two strands of floss throughout except for the cloud around the moon which is a single strand of 826.

Stem stitch is used for the majority of the work, apart from the reindeers' legs which are back stitch (when they get thin), the fur on Santa's hat and his beard which are worked in long and short stitch at angles to the lines of the pattern to give a sort of rough effect.

NOTE: Remember Rudolph's red nose!!

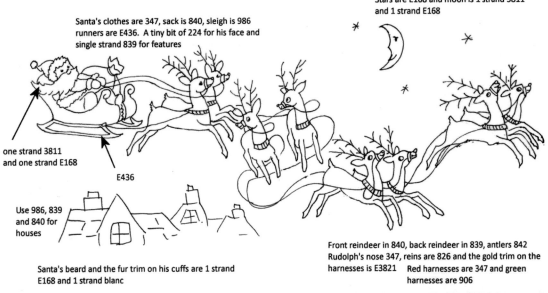

Santa's clothes are 347, sack is 840, sleigh is 986 runners are E436. A tiny bit of 224 for his face and single strand 839 for features

Stars are E168 and moon is 1 strand 3811 and 1 strand E168

one strand 3811 and one strand E168

E436

Use 986, 839 and 840 for houses

Santa's beard and the fur trim on his cuffs are 1 strand E168 and 1 strand blanc

Front reindeer in 840, back reindeer in 839, antlers 842 Rudolph's nose 347, reins are 826 and the gold trim on the harnesses is E3821   Red harnesses are 347 and green harnesses are 906

When your embroidery panel is finished, press gently on the reverse and put to one side.

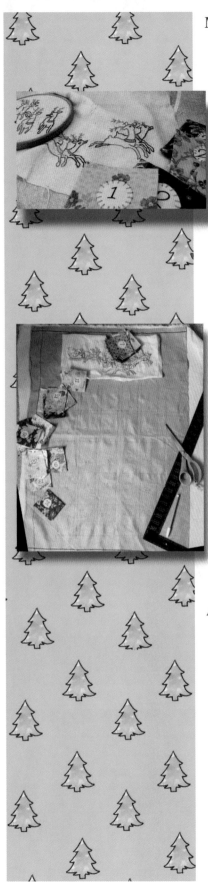

Make your pockets:

- Print the numbers on page 14 onto your white cotton fabric, or stitch/stamp numbers onto suitable fabric.

- Cut around the circle lines and stitch one number onto each 5" square of quilting fabric, positioning your number in the centre vertically and 1" down from the top edge.

- To attach use 3 strands of E436 and straight stitches, worked at right angles to the edges of the circles.

- Fold ¼" under along the top of each 5" square and press.

- Fold 1" under on each side and press.

- Fold 1 ¼" under at bottom of each 5" square and press.

- Make ½" pinch pleat at the centre bottom of each pocket and tack into place.

- Position your pockets on your main panel. This needs to be accurate as if they are wonky then your eye will be instantly drawn to this. It is easiest to draw a grid on your fabric panel using your erasable fabric marker.

- Centre your middle pocket over the centre of the fabric, then draw your grid as shown on the left. The space for each pocket is 2 ½" wide x 3 ½" high and you should leave a ¼" gap between pockets horizontally and 1" gap between pockets vertically.

- Position your pockets on the squares and pin or tack in place, then topstitch around the sides and bottom, leaving the top open. Erase all visible grid lines.

Assemble your calendar:

- Turn under and press ½" on all sides of your embroidery. Position at top of calendar with lace below to form border, mitering corners. Tack, then machine in place.

- With your erasable marker print "Twas the night before Christmas ..." at the bottom of your calendar, 1" below the bottom of the pockets. Embroider in chain stitch using 3 strands of 986.

- Place front panel on top of canvas and machine stitch around the edges ¼" from the edge.

- Cover this stitching with bias binding. Stitch 2 rings on the back for hanging.

- Fill pockets and enjoy!!

Decorate your Home

Capture the spirit of Christmas and enjoy the weeks leading up to the holidays by making your own decorations to adorn your home over the festive period.

Really nice, ethically made ornaments are expensive to purchase and it's much nicer to make your own - perhaps with the help of the younger members of your family. You'll create your own unique selection of goodies - ones that nobody else in the whole wide world will have, and that are sure to be admired by your visitors.

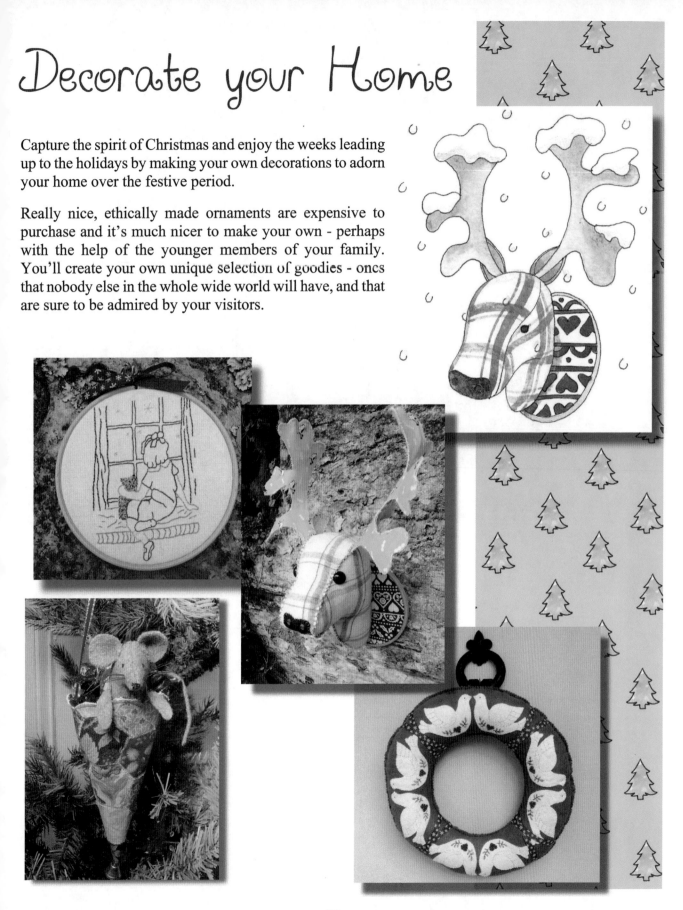

Star of Wonder

Rosie and Bear are sitting on the old window-seat gazing up at the clear starry sky - perhaps they're hoping to spot Santa and Rudolph making their Christmas Eve deliveries?!

Shown mounted in a 6" hoop.

You will need:

- 8" square neutral coloured cotton, linen or cotton/linen blend fabric suitable for embroidery
- DMC stranded cotton floss in colours: 310, 315, 433, 504, 561, 676, 680, 826, 989, 3774, 3845, 3862, 4065, E168, blanc

Notes on working:

- Use two strands of floss throughout.

- Bear's eye and nose are worked in 310 (black floss) with the tiniest little stitch of white to give his eye a bit of sparkle.

- Stars are worked in star stitch in E168

- If you haven't stitched Bear before - then don't worry, fur is really easy when you know how. Just download my free guide "How to Embroider Fur" for all the help you'll need to make your Bear look really furry!

Stitch Guide:

561 stem stitch

826 back stitch

Bear's fur is worked in a mixture of 676 (light), 680 (med) and 433 (dark) brown straight stitches. Ribbon satin stitch 4065

3845 back stitch

349 back stitch

3862 back stitch

989 back stitch

349 stem stitch

3774 back stitch

504 back stitch
315 back stitch

31

Fabric Reindeer Head

Cute little mounted reindeer head - enjoy the look without any worries about animal cruelty!   He's mounted on a 6" hoop and measures 14" from the bottom of his neck to the tips of his antlers.

This reindeer will make a great addition to your Christmas decorations - and I'm tempted to make another in tweed and linen to display all year round!

You will need:

12" square woollen/felt fabric for head
18" x 9" quilting weight cotton fabric for antlers
9" square canvas or heavy interfacing for antlers
2 x 13mm safety eyes
Small scrap of pink fabric/felt for inners of ears
2" square scrap fabric for nose
8" square medium weight fabric for hoop
8" square card to back hoop
Brown and blue stranded cotton embroidery floss
2 x ¼" buttons for nostrils.
Toy stuffing
22" length galvanised garden wire
Temporary fabric spray adhesive
Temporary fabric marker pen
Hot glue gun (you can use PVA glue but allow for drying time)
6" wooden embroidery hoop

To make the antlers:

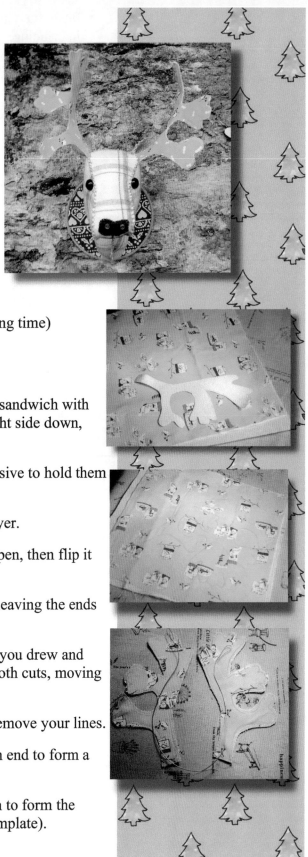

- Cut your cotton fabric into two 9" squares. Make a sandwich with the interfacing/canvas as follows: Cotton fabric right side down, interfacing/canvas, cotton fabric right side up.

- Lightly spray the layers with temporary fabric adhesive to hold them together.

- Take your antler template and place it on the top layer.

- Draw around it with your temporary fabric marker pen, then flip it over and draw around it again.

- Machine stitch all along the lines you have drawn, leaving the ends open.

- Now cut out your antlers. Cut ¼" outside the lines you drew and stitched over. Use large shears and make long smooth cuts, moving the fabric rather than the shears.

- Machine zig-zag around the edges of the antlers. Remove your lines.

- Take your galvanised wire and bend over 1" at each end to form a loop.

- Bend the wire into a "U" shape and then bend again to form the antler shape (indicated by the dotted lines on the template).

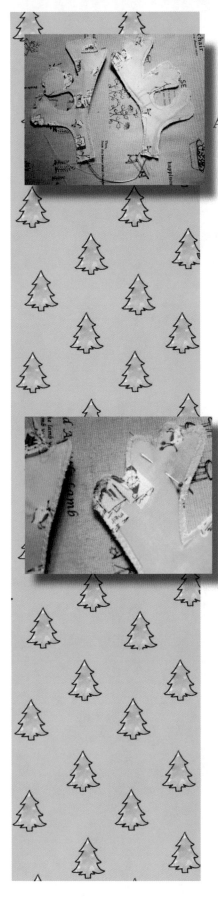

- Push the wire up into the antler shapes between the cotton and interfacing.

- Pin into place through all layers of fabric/interfacing and the wire loops

Assemble the Head:

- Cut out the two head pieces, one gusset and four ear pieces.

- Place a felt and pink fabric ear piece wrong sides together and stitch around three edges using cross stitch (work half in one direction, then turn around and come back the other way). Don't stitch the bottom of the ear as this will be hidden within the head.

- Place the ears to one side for the moment.

- Using the template as a guide, mark the positions of the eyes with your pen.

- Stitch the two sides of the neck in the same way together with wrong sides together from A to C.

- Now insert the gusset. Stitch up both sides of the head from A to the first X marking the position of the antlers.

- Stuff the nose part of the head

- Place the antlers so that the bottom of the "U" shape is inside the head and then add more stuffing around the U.

- This is a bit fiddly, but now you need to stitch the antlers into place within the seams. Do each side in turn, holding firmly in place, . Don't worry if they flop forwards, you can easily re-position them and when you complete stuffing the head they will remain in place.

- Continue along each side seam to the X marking the position of the ears.

- Fold your ear shape in half vertically with the pink side innermost, then stitch into the seam.

- Insert the safety eyes before completing the stitching.

- Complete stitching to the back of the neck.

- Now, holding the antlers in their correct position, stuff the head very firmly, moulding the stuffing all around the "U" shape at the bottom of the wire.

- Close the back seam from B to C adding more stuffing if needed as you go. The head must be stuffed firmly or the antlers will flop forward and it won't sit properly on the hoop.

- Cut a nose shape from your brown fabric and stitch into place on the head. Embroider the mouth and add two small buttons for the nostrils.

- The head is now finished.

Assemble the mounted head:

- Place your medium weight fabric in the hoop, if it's directional then make sure it's straight and the right way up (the screw will be at the top of the hoop).

- Screw as tightly as you can. Trim fabric to within ½" of edge of hoop, press under and hold in place with glue.

- Cut a circle of card to fit the inside of the hoop and glue in place.

- Now take your reindeer head and run a line of glue right the way down the back seam and spread it either side so that it covers about ½" strip at the back of the neck.

- Press neck very firmly against the fabric in the hoop and hold into place until the glue has set.

- The head is very light and this should be all that is necessary to sit it firmly upon the mount.

- If your head does flop forward, then you can push a sharp bamboo skewer through from the back of the hoop and up into the neck and then glue the other end into place at the back of the hoop, but this shouldn't really be necessary.

FINISHED!!

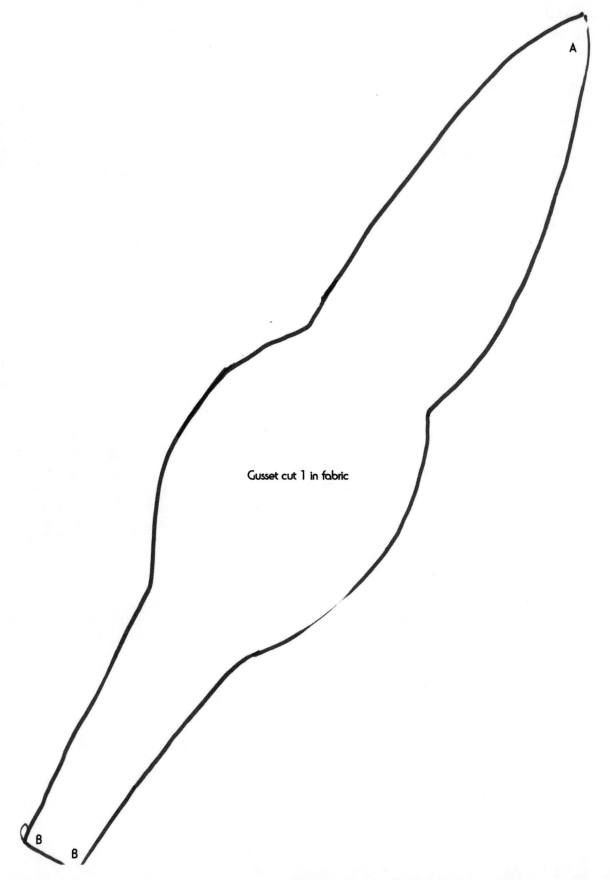

Gusset cut 1 in fabric

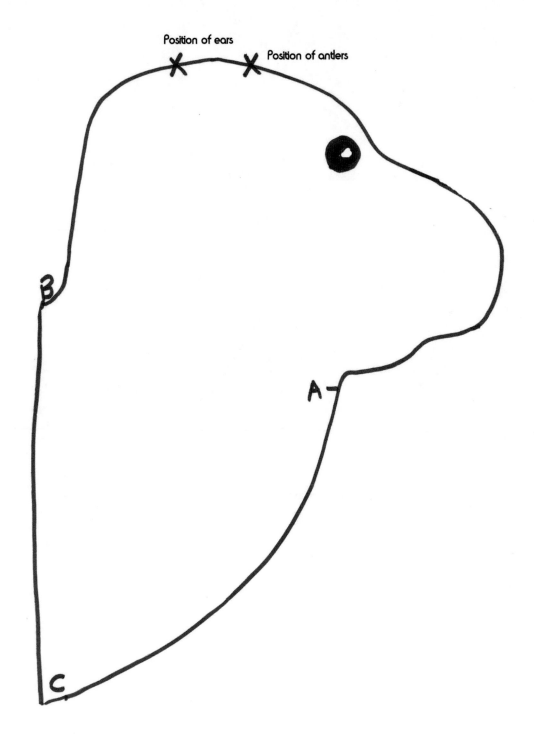

Position of ears

Position of antlers

B

A —

C

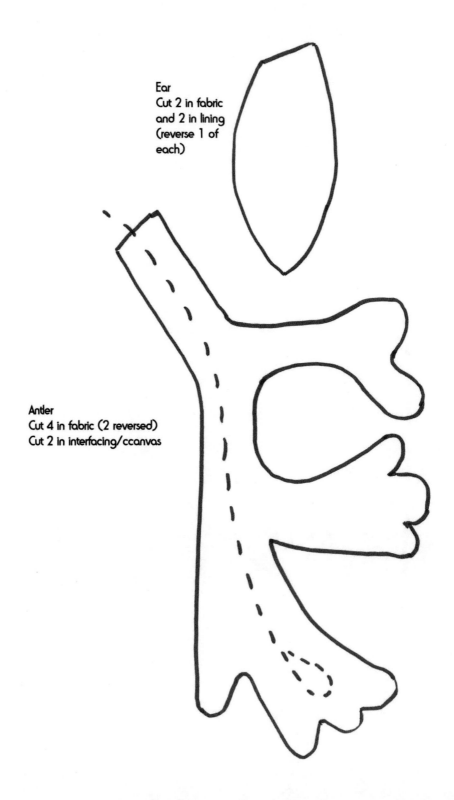

Ear
Cut 2 in fabric
and 2 in lining
(reverse 1 of
each)

Antler
Cut 4 in fabric (2 reversed)
Cut 2 in interfacing/ccanvas

Candy Cone Mouse

This little mouse and his cone measure 8" long from the bottom of the Cone (excluding bell) to the tip of mouse's ears.

Fill his cone with candy and little mouse will resist every temptation to nibble before Christmas morning!

- With the right side uppermost, take your fabric hexagons and arrange them over the top of the cone shape. You will need to use a few of the little scraps left over from cutting your hexagons to cover some of the edges completely.

- When you are happy with the arrangement, secure them to the canvas using your spray fabric adhesive.

- Thread your sewing machine with the gold machine thread. Bobbin colour doesn't really matter. Set on a wide zig-zag with short stitch length (as if you were making buttonholes)

- Zig-zag over where all the hexagon edges meet.

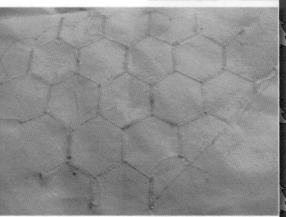

- Flip over so you can see your markings on the reverse and cut out your cone shape.

- Now I am a very bad cutter, so rather than cut out my cone lining separately and risk the scallops being different shapes, I do it this way: Lay your felt square on a clean flat surface. Spray the back of your cut-out cone shape with fabric adhesive and press down onto the felt square. Cut around the cone shape (hey-presto – matching scallops!!)

- Making sure you have red thread in your bobbin and gold in your needle, machine button-hole stitch over the scallop edges with the patchwork side uppermost. Set your zig-zag at its widest as this is a nice decorative detail.

- Fold your cone in half lengthways and machine stitch along seam. (I know this leaves the edges showing on the inside, but fraying isn't really an issue here, and the inside will be concealed by the candy).

You will need:

- 5   x 5" squares of quilting weight fabric in Christmassy patterns for cone. (Note: If you don't want to make the hexagonal patchwork, then you could use crazy patchwork or just a single 12" square of fabric)
- 12" square piece of medium weight canvas or heavy-weight non-fusible interfacing
- 12" square red felt for lining
- Gold machine thread
- Red bobbin thread
- 6" square grey felt (or felted blanket/other material)
- 2   x ¼" white buttons for shoulders
- 1   x ½" red button for base of tail
- Black embroidery floss for features
- Dark brown strong thread for whiskers
- Small quantity of toy stuffing
- 16" length ¼" wide ribbon for hanging cone
- Small bell for base of cone (optional)
- Black sharpie or other thick marker pen
- Fabric adhesive

To make cone:

- Cut 20" hexagons with 1" sides from your quilting fabric and put to one side for now.

- Using the template at the end of the pattern, draw your cone shape onto your canvas or interfacing with your thick marker pen. Flip it over at the fold mark so you draw a complete cone shape. DO NOT CUT IT OUT. Make sure you can see the line on the other side of the fabric.

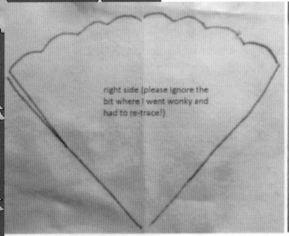

right side (please ignore the bit where I went wonky and had to re-trace!)

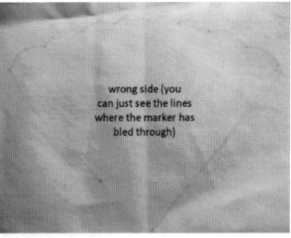

wrong side (you can just see the lines where the marker has bled through)

Make the mouse:

- Cut out all mouse pieces using the template at the end of the pattern. Depending on which method you prefer to join the pieces (see next step) you may need to add ¼" seam allowance to the body pieces.

- Additionally cut a strip of felt 5" x ¼" for his tail. Give this strip a nice pointy end.

- Sew the head and body shape together. I have another cheat's way of cutting small toy pieces to overcome my poor cutting skills … draw around template on one piece of felt, then place on top of second and pin. Stitch pieces together around line and then cut out. No slipping or distortion of small pieces!! If you prefer to cut and then stitch, please add ¼" seam allowance to the pattern.

- Turn right side out and stuff the head, neck and top part of the body firmly, and the bottom of the body quite lightly, stopping your stuffing ½" from the bottom.

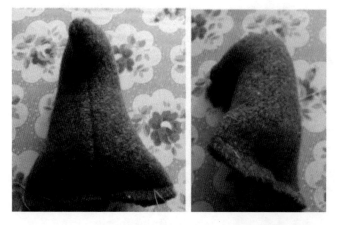

- With front and back seams matching, stitch along bottom edge of mouse. (this edge will be hidden inside the cone).

- Attach arms, adding small button at shoulders. Form a curve by overlapping the sides of the notch at the bottom of the ear shapes and stitch into place on the head.

- Attach tail to base of body and secure with red button (sorry I forgot to take a picture of wip but I think you can see here).

- Add features and whiskers to mouse.

- Position mouse in cone and stitch or glue in place with his arms overlapping the cone edges and his tail hanging over the side.

- Attach ribbon to inside of cone edges for hanging and add small bell at the pointy tip of the cone.

- Note: before filling with candy, you might like to add a little stuffing at the bottom to help the cone keep its nice pointy shape.

- When adding candy, be sure to move his tail out of the way and then drape across the top of the sweets as though he'd just climbed in!

Dove of Peace Wreath

Felt is a wonderful medium to work with at Christmas - it's so easy to use and there is such a wonderful choice of colours available. Just three colours are used in this applique wreath - the traditional Christmas colours of red, green and white.

Finished wreath measures 15" diameter.

You will need:

- 18" square green felt
- 18" square red felt
- 12" square white felt
- 2" x 3" red felt
- 1 ½ yards ½" wide Christmas ribbon
- 1" curtain ring to hang
- Stranded cotton embroidery floss in white, silver, green, brown, very dark blue and pale pink
- Green thread for your machine needle and red for the bobbin
- Temporary fabric spray adhesive or Bondaweb
- Pinking shears (optional, but nice)
- Ruler
- Temporary fabric marker pen

Applique Doves:

- Take your 18" square green felt and fold in half lengthways and across. Where the folds cross is the centre of the piece, mark the centre.

- Using your ruler, measure a circle of 8 ½" diameter centred upon the fabric. Mark this circle with your temporary fabric marker pen.

- Using the templates on the following page (supplied actual size) cut 8 dove shapes, 4 facing right and 4 facing left.

- Position these dove shapes on your green felt, aligning their breasts with the 8 ½" circle you drew. You may need to shift them around a little until you're happy with the spacing. When you are, then secure in place with Bondaweb or fabric adhesive.

- With your temporary fabric marker pen draw lines for embroidery onto doves.

- Cut 8 heart shapes from red felt and fuse to doves.

- Work embroidery on dove shapes as follows using 2 strands of floss throughout:

- Secure dove shapes to background with small straight stitches in 2 strands of white floss. The stitches should be at right-angles to the applique.

- Work wings and tail lines in back stitch using silver floss. Work 2 or 3 small straight stitches over the beaks.

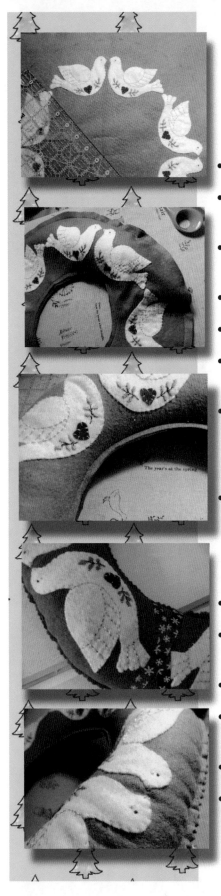

- Work leaves in satin stitch using green floss and stems in back stitch in brown floss

- Secure each heart with small straight stitches using silver floss.

- The eyes are tiny French knots in dark blue floss and cheeks two or three satin stitches in pale pink floss.

- Press your applique lightly on the reverse.

- Now draw two circles, centred on the mark you made at the beginning. These circles should be 6" and 16" diameter.

- Cut out along the lines - you will now have a doughnut-shaped ring. Cut the same shape in your red felt for the back of your wreath.

- Place the two shapes together, right sides outwards and pin in place.

- Machine stitch all around the inner circle, ½" from the edge.

- Machine stitch ¼ of the way around the outer circle, again ½" from the edge.

- Insert toy stuffing into stitched part of wreath, then sew the next quarter of the outside edge - stop and stuff that bit - you're stuffing as you go around which is so much easier than trying to stuff this shape at the end.

- Continue until wreath is nearly stuffed. The stuffing should be packed in quite firmly - insert it in small tufts to avoid getting lumps in your wreath and push well into place with your fingers or a stuffing stick (bamboo skewer with the end broken off and frayed so it will hold onto the stuffing).

- Close the gap by hand.

- Trim around the inner and outer edges of your wreath with pinking shears to within ¼" of your stitching line.

- Cut your Christmas ribbon into 8 pieces

- Cross across the front of the wreath between the doves' tails and secure at the back with a few stitches.

- Stitch hanging ring to top back of wreath.

- Hang and enjoy!

49

Christmas Softies

These little creatures will love to join your family at Christmas time - and they make great gift ideas too. After all, who could possibly resist an Angel Pig, Carol Singing Mouse or even a plump little Christmas Goose complete with woolly hat and scarf?

These softies are not designed to be toys, and the designs given here are not suitable for young children. Having said that though ,with some modfications (eg stitching eyes instead of using beads) they could be adapted for older children to enjoy as much as us grown-ups!

Carol Singing Mice

These little mice are really easy to make - why limit yourself to a pair? What about a trio - or a whole choir even? Using a glue gun for part of the project makes for quick assembly and you'll even find their little song-books at the end of this pattern - just print and glue or stitch onto their front paws.

The Christmas trees are really easy too - just polystyrene cones covered in green fabric with buttons glued to them. The bottom of the fabric was trimmed with pinking shears to make a nice edge. The bases are old cotton reels with red fabric wrapped round them glued to the bases of the cones.

For one mouse - you will need

- 6" square in light brown or other suitable colour felt for mouse fur
- 2" square piece of light card
- Stranded cotton floss or Perle thread in toning colour for seams
- Black cotton floss for nose and eyes
- Strong brown thread for whiskers
- 6" length of string for tail
- Strip of felt ¾" x 9" for scarf
- Toy stuffing
- Hot glue gun (optional)
- Needle and thread

To make mouse

- Cut out template pieces and position on felt.

- Cut 1 head piece, 2 body pieces, 2 ear pieces, 4 arm pieces, 1 base and 2 feet. Cut a second base in cardboard, using the dotted line on the template as guide.

- With right sides together and ordinary thread stitch darts at side of head using back stitch.

- Turn right sides out and with wrong sides together join seams from nose to neck and down back of head. Use 2 strands of floss or medium Perle thread and cross or blanket stitch over seams to give a nice finish. Stuff **head.** Use very small pieces of stuffing and push well down nose. Put head to one side.

- Place body pieces wrong sides together and stitch seams in cross or blanket stitch as before.

- Turn inside out so wrong side is on the outside.

- Push head up inside body, aligning seams at neck, then join head to body with thread and back stitch. (doing it this way gives a nice smooth join on the outside so you won't have a ridge showing under the scarf).

- Stuff body firmly, then stitch base into place using cross or blanket stitch. When you're half-way round slip your cardboard base inside body, between felt base and stuffing. This will ensure your mice has a nice flat bottom so he will stand up without wobbling.

- Push the end of the piece of string inside at the back seam and stitch into place for the tail.

- Trim string to desired length and knot at the end to prevent fraying.

- Place 2 arm pieces together and cross or blanket stitch around edges leaving a gap at the middle bottom for stuffing. (It's easier to stuff such a small piece from the middle).

- Stuff firmly and close gap. Repeat for second arm. Put to one side for a moment.

- Sew ear darts with needle and thread using back stitch. Position ears and when you're happy with the position, stitch to head.

- With black embroidery floss make a few small stitches for each eye. It's a good idea to mark position of eyes with pins first - try a few different positions until you're happy with how your mouse looks.

- Stitch over end of nose for his nose.

- Use strong thread for whiskers. Take small stitches beneath his black nose to secure whiskers in place.

- Tie scarf around neck and trim ends to desired length. Make small vertical cuts in ends to represent fringes.

- Print mouse song-book (a heavier weight paper is best if you have it), cut out and fix to mouse paws using a thin line of glue down the edges where his paws will touch the book.

- Finished!!

Christmas Songs

Music arranged for mice

* Cut felt base along solid line and card insert along dotted line

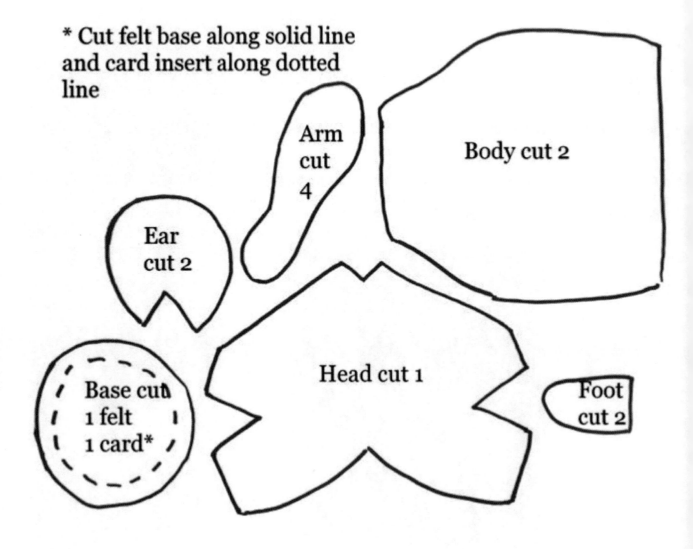

Arm cut 4

Body cut 2

Ear cut 2

Base cut 1 felt 1 card*

Head cut 1

Foot cut 2

Angel Pigs

These little pigs look far too solid to be real angel pigs .... more as though they have rummaged around in their dressing-up box and found some wings to attach to their plump little bodies. They are really easy to make – most of the sewing is done by hand, apart from the wings which I have sewn by machine, though you could hand stitch these if you wanted.

Instructions/quantities in this pattern are to make one pig only and the template is actual size (though of course you can make your pigs any size you want!).

There are no seam allowances for the pig's body and the wings have a ¼" seam allowance included in the pattern.

You will need:

- 12" square of felt in your chosen colour for the pig's body
- 6" square piece of light-weight fabric for the wings.
- 1   small button for nose
- 12" ribbon to wrap around body
- Small amount black and pink embroidery floss for eye and cheeks
- Embroidery floss to stitch pig – choose a colour that will work well with the felt you have
- chosen for the body.
- Hairspray & a pencil
- Stuffing

To make your pig:

- Cut all your pieces using the template at the end of this pattern.

- Using blanket stitch and two strands of floss, stitch underbelly pieces to main body pieces from A to B around legs and trotters.

- Now attach the top gusset on one side. Start at point A and carefully ease the gusset around the pig's snout. Then continue up and over the back and round to his bum.

- Attach the second main body to the top gusset in the same way. It's very important that you are accurate, particularly matching A as otherwise he'll have a wonky snout! Keep checking all looks well as you stitch around his snout.

- Using ladder stitch close the gap between his underbelly pieces for 1 ½" back and front. This should leave a large enough gap for stuffing.

- Stuff your pig's body firmly, pushing the stuffing well down into his legs and snout, moulding and squeezing as you go to achieve the best shape. Only insert small pieces at a time to avoid lumpiness. Then close the gap with ladder stitch.

- Fold the ears in half vertically and secure at base with a few stitches. Position them on the sides of the head and stitch into place using thread that matches your felt.

- Stitch eyes and cheeks (you may find it helpful to use a glass-headed pin to discover the right positions - try several until you like your pig's expression). Make sure the eyes are level!

- Stitch small button onto the end of the pig's snout.

- Place your wing pieces right sides together and machine stitch around edges, leaving a gap for turning and stuffing as shown below.

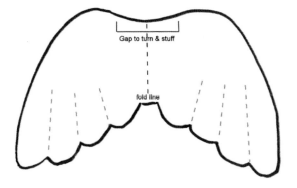

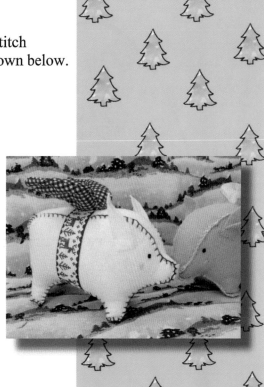

- Turn right side out and stuff lightly. Stitch gap closed.

- Machine or hand stitch along red dotted lines on diagram above to represent wing feathers.

- Fold in half along black dotted line in diagram and machine stitch from front to back of wings ¼" from fold. This will give your pig's wings a nice "lift".

- Position wings on the pig's back and when you're happy with them, stitch into place.

- Wrap ribbon around pig from one side of wings to the other, folding under at the wing edge to help disguise your wing stitches.

- Finally for the tail - attach perle or floss at the base of the pig's back leaving a 1 ½" long thread loose. Wrap this thread around a pencil, securing the end with sticky tape.

- Spray liberally with hairspray to set. When set, carefully remove the sticky tape and pencil leaving a nice curly tail.

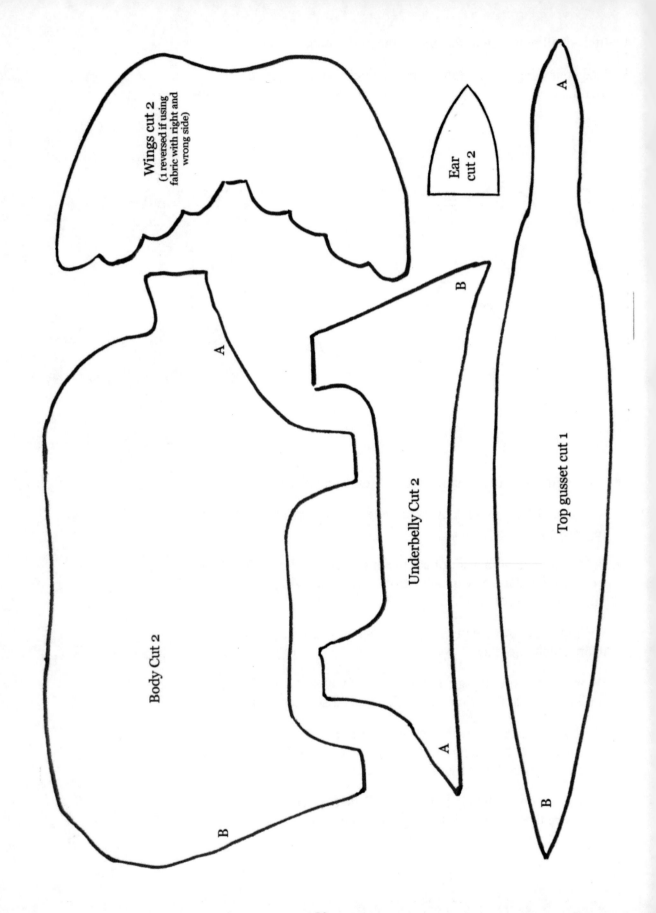

Wings cut 2
(1 reversed if using fabric with right and wrong side)

Ear cut 2

A

B

A

Top gusset cut 1

B

Underbelly Cut 2

A

B

A

Body Cut 2

B

Christmas Geese

These little geese stand about 10" high and are a great way to use up scraps of fabric and odd buttons. Make them in linen, or felt/woollen fabric scraps work just as well too.

A great Christmas decorating idea!

Not suitable for young children due to use of wire and pebbles.

You will need

- 1 Fat Quarter main fabric (but you won't need all of this, a Fat Eighth will work with careful positioning of the pieces)
- Oddments of contrast fabric – one piece must measure 8" long (20 cm) 4"(10 cm) square of yellow felt for legs
- Oddment of lighter felt for beak (or you can use the same as the legs)
- Two ¾" buttons (optional)
- 2 x 6" (15 cm) lengths of garden wire to support legs
- Embroidery floss in black and another colour
- Thread or floss the same colour as the felt you're using for the legs
- Two smooth pebbles, each about 1 -1 ½ inch long (2.5 – 3 cm) Toy stuffing
- Tiny black beads for eyes (optional)

To make your goose:

- First cut out your pieces using the template on the last page. You need to cut one body shape with the template the right side up, then reverse it to cut the second shape. Do the same with the wing template so you have a pair of wings. The template is shown actual size and ¼" seam allowance is included in the pieces

- Place one side of the gusset against the main body between the point marked "X" on the template and the tip of the tail. Stitch together.

- Repeat with the other side, then stitch all around the body leaving a 3" gap at the top for stuffing.

- Clip curves and trim away excess fabric at point of tail (careful not to cut through stitching)

- Then turn right side out and stuff firmly, positioning the pebbles at the base of the bird – these will weight the body at the bottom and help keep your goose standing. I've shown the positioning of the pebbles on the picture above. Make sure they're well cushioned with stuffing so they don't rattle around!

- Slip stitch the gap closed.

- Pair up the wings – the outer is the contrast fabric and the inner is main fabric. Place each pair of pieces right side together, and machine around the edges, leaving a 1 ½ " gap along the top edge for stuffing.

- Clip curves, trim point of wing, turn right side out and stuff lightly. Slip stitch the gap closed.

- Fold the beak piece in half, and stitch along curved seam. Turn right side out and stuff.

Assemble your bird:

- Position the beak at the front of the head and top stitch into place.

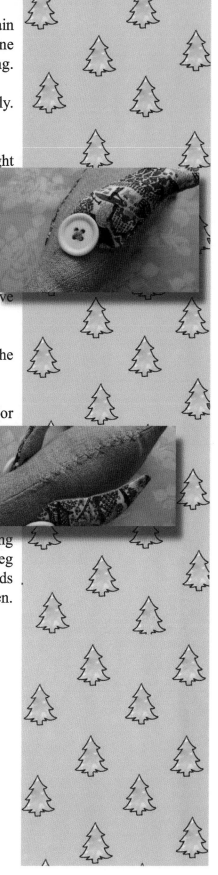

- Position wings, stitch into place along front edge and add decorative button using embroidery floss for a nice effect.

- Using 3 strands of floss, add some decorative cross stitch over the opening you slip stitched closed earlier.

- Stitch the eyes using black floss and a few small stitches. (or alternatively if preferred you could use tiny black beads)

Add the legs:

- Take a length of wire and bend it into a loop.

- Place on top of one of the legs as shown and stitch into place using matching thread or floss. It doesn't matter what the back of the leg and the bottom of the foot look like as they won't be seen. The ends of the wire will stick out (see photo below) - you want this to happen.

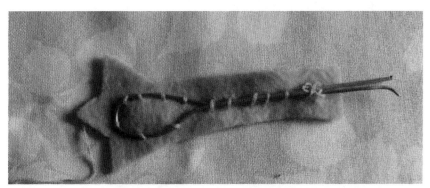

- Then place the second piece of felt on top and stitch together around all edges.

- Above is the front and the picture below shows how the back looks.

- Turn the goose body upside down and hold it firmly. Now take one leg and, with the front of the leg against the body, push the two wire ends into the body so that they are no longer visible.

- You should push the wire in at a shallow angle so that the leg is snug against the body. Now stitch around the top ½" (1 cm) of the leg through the felt, securing it firmly to the body.

- Bend the leg away from the body at a right angle.

- Now catch the sides of the felt leg and top stitch them together at the back. This has the effect of narrowing the leg

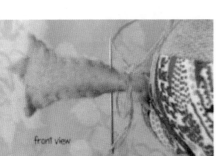

- Do this all the way down until the leg starts to widen out into the foot shape

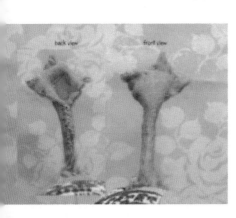

- Here you can see what the front and back of the leg should look like

- Repeat with the second leg. Then bend the feet backwards at right-angles to the leg and stand your goose up.

And you're finished!! You can give your geese a different look by making him or her in felt or blanket. like the one on the following page. He is hand stitched with cross stitch – worked half cross stitch in one direction, returning the other way so his seams are on the outside of his body.

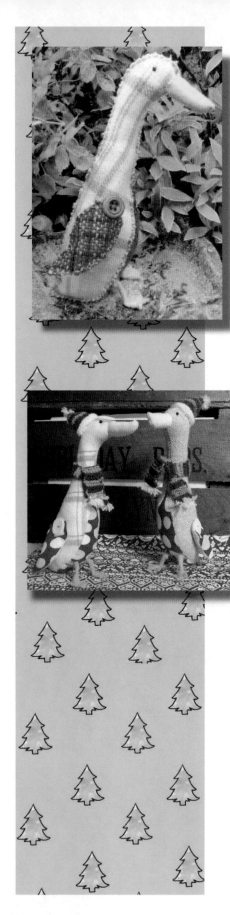

Or you could knit him a little hat and scarf as shown in the image below. Here's how you do this:

You will need:

1 pair 2.75 mm (UK 12, US2) needles

Small amounts of red, white and blue or green 4 ply yarn (or colours of your choice)

For Scarf:

Cast on 7 stitches and work 6" in garter stitch in stripes of 4 rows. Cast off. With a large needle add white yarn for fringes (make loopy stitches kept in place with small back stitches). Fluff fringe and tie scarf around neck.

For Hat:

Cast on 25 stitches in white yarn and work 10 rows in garter stitch.
Change to red yarn and work 4 rows in stocking stitch
Change to green/blue yarn and work 2 rows in stocking stitch
Change to red yarn and work 4 rows in stocking stitch
Change to green/blue yarn. (K1, K2tog) eight times, K1.
Purl one row.
Change to red yarn. (K1, K2tog) to end of row. Purl one row.
Work 2 rows in stocking stitch.
Change to blue/green yarn and work 2 rows in stocking stitch.
Change to red yarn and K2tog to end of row, Purl 1 row

Thread yarn through remaining stitches and pull up tightly.

Sew up back seam of hat, pulling the yarn slightly as you sew so that the hat will fold over slightly. Fold up garter stitch edging and slip stitch in place.

Position hat on goose's head and when happy with positioning slip stitch into place.

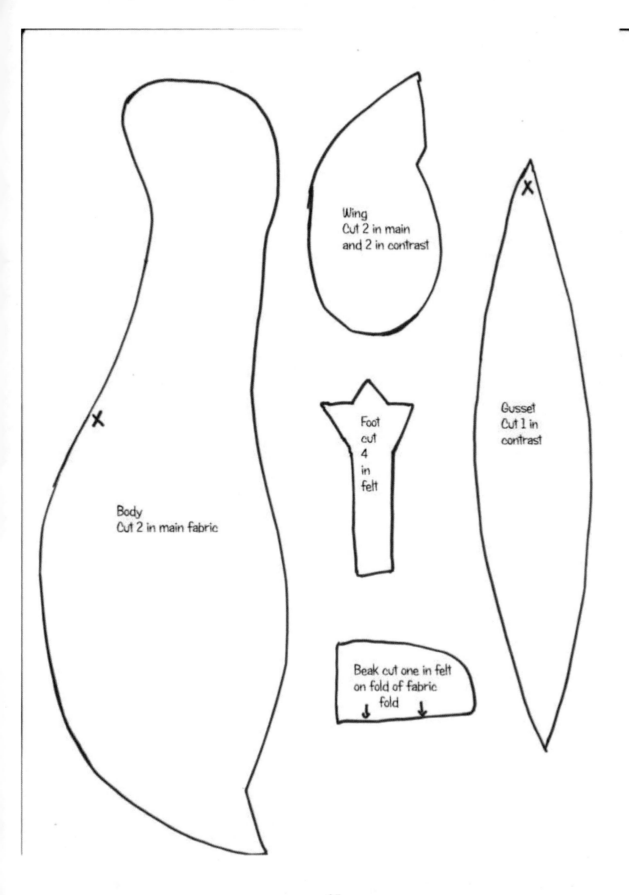

Wing
Cut 2 in main
and 2 in contrast

Gusset
Cut 1 in
contrast

Foot
cut
4
in
felt

Body
Cut 2 in main fabric

Beak cut one in felt
on fold of fabric
fold

Soft Furnishings

In all the rush and frantic activity leading up to Christmas Day, it's easy to become stressed and forget to take time to enjoy the holiday period yourself.

On the next pages you'll find some seasonal cushion covers that will encourage you to sit down, put your feet up and enjoy a few moments peace and quiet - and possibly even some stitching too - before returning refreshed to your preparations, as well as a delightful table runner that will look wonderful on your dining room table over Christmas

Nordic Reindeer Cushion

I have always loved the trend for Nordic style at Christmas - taking inspiration from the landscape and natural motifs like stars, snowflakes - and reindeer of course!

And the colour scheme - red, white and green. Nordic style is easy to create in your own home this Christmas with this simple, but very effective cushion-cover, why not make a pair - you'll be finished in under a day!

Dimensions are given for a 16" pad, but for larger or smaller simply resize the template accordingly.

You will need:

- 16" x 24" piece of cream wool felt or blanket
- 12" x 8" red felt for reindeer
- 16" x 1" strip green felt for bottom border
- 4" square green felt for heart
- 16" red ric rac braid
- 16" x 4" strip red and white fabric for top and bottom borders of cushion cover
- ¾" cream button
- Bondaweb
- Cream and red DMC Perle no.5
- Invisible thread for your machine needle, light colour in the bobbin
- Pinking shears (optional)

Make cushion front

- Take your cream fabric and cut into three 16" x 12" rectangles.

- Put two of the the rectangles to one side for the moment.

- Cut your strip of red and white fabric in half lengthways, then sew to the long edges of your cream fabric rectangle.

- Press seams at the back.

- Take your strip of green felt and cut one side into points (see photo for guide) using your pinking shears if you have them.

- Position on your cushion front with the bottom edge of the strip 1" up from your seam.

- Baste or pin, then machine stitch in two straight lines - one across the points and one along the bottom - using invisible thread. (You can use green thread and pivot on the points if you prefer - but I wanted this to be a quick and easy decorative make for Christmas).

- Trace your reindeer shapes onto the Bondaweb (1 reversed) iron to the back of the felt and cut out.

- Position your reindeer on the cushion front ½" up from your green strip. Their noses should be 1 ½" apart.

- When you're happy with their positioning, iron into place.

- Cut a heart shape from your green felt with your pinking shears. The shape should measure 3" across at the widest point.

- Cut a slightly smaller heart in cream felt.

- Stitch your red ric-rac braid along the top of the cushion 1 ¾" down from your seam. Invisible thread is good for this too.

- Position the heart shapes on top of the ric-rac braid (see photo for guide) and stitch into place.

- Now with your perle thread, stitch cross-stitches and French knots in red along your pointy green strip and cross stitches/running stitch on your heart shapes (see photo for guide).

- Secure your reindeer shapes with small stitches in cream perle thread and then stitch a star with straight stitches on each reindeer - the position is shown on the template.

- Stitch button into place in centre of hearts.

Assemble your cushion:

- With your red perle thread, blanket stitch over one of the shorter sides of each cream felt rectangle.

- Lay the front of your cushion right side up on a clean flat surface.

- Place one of the back pieces on top of this, right side down, aligning the side edge and with the blanket stitched edge towards the centre.

- Place the second back piece along the opposite side edge.

- Pin or tack the pieces in place.

- Stitch all around the edges of the cushion, then trim with pinking shears. Cut excess from corners.

- Turn right side out through the back opening.

- Insert your cushion pad.

FINISHED!!

Starry Nights Embroidery

Simple embroidery for you to enjoy - either mount and hang - or why not make into a cushion cover with some simple log cabin patchwork as I have here.

The only stitches used are French knots and back or straight stitch.

Finished embroidery measures 6" x 7".

The instructions for working the embroidery follow - I have turned my completed panel into a cushion cover using a simple log cabin pattern and 2" wide blocks. My deer wasn't quite square, so a little trimming was needed at top and bottom, but this wasn't noticeable in the finished cushion. I quilted the cushion front - stitching in the ditch around the embroidery and along the top of the snowy hill, then stippled the log cabin blocks.

For the embroidery only:

You will need:

8" square cream linen or other fabric suitable for embroidery

8" x 4" rectangle dark blue linen

DMC stranded cotton embroidery floss in colours: E168, 310,522, 598, 841, 3750, 3781, 3790, 3813, 3863, 3864, 4065, blanc, ecru

Notes on working:

Use 2 strands of floss throughout.

I have given the templates actual size and also reversed to suit your preferred method of transfer. Transfer the whole design to your cream fabric, as this will ensure that you have the correct positioning of the line for the snowy hill.

Work the embroidery according to the stitch guide on the following page.

The design shows the lines for stitching the deer's fur - you can add extra stitches to those shown.

Study the photo in the stitch guide carefully so you can see where I have used the different browns - darker on the lower sides of the leg and side, and around the head. Just imagine how the light would be falling on the deer and this will make it easy to decide where the darker browns (or shadows) should be used.

The deer's eye is worked in satin stitch 310 surrounded by small straight stitches in 3781 and a highlight of two tiny stitches in blanc. The nose is worked in the same way.

The rabbits are easy to stitch in back stitch and the eyes are 310 with a blanc highlight. Don't make the noses black - this is too harsh, they need to be 3781 dark brown.

I have worked the tails in Turkey knot, but you could use French knots if you prefer.

The snow is all worked in French knots, mix the colours around the deer and rabbits, and include a little E168. Vary the size of the knots between one and two twists if you like. The hill behind the deer is all 3813 in single twist knots.

When your embroidery is completed, trim your cream fabric ¼ " above the line of the snowy hill and press this seam allowance under, clipping if necessary.

Place your cream fabric on top of the navy blue 3 ½" down from the top on the left hand side. Then and pin or tack together, and slip stitch your hill to the navy fabric.

Work your stars - only the large star is shown on the template, but I decided to add some smaller ones as well.

Press lightly on reverse

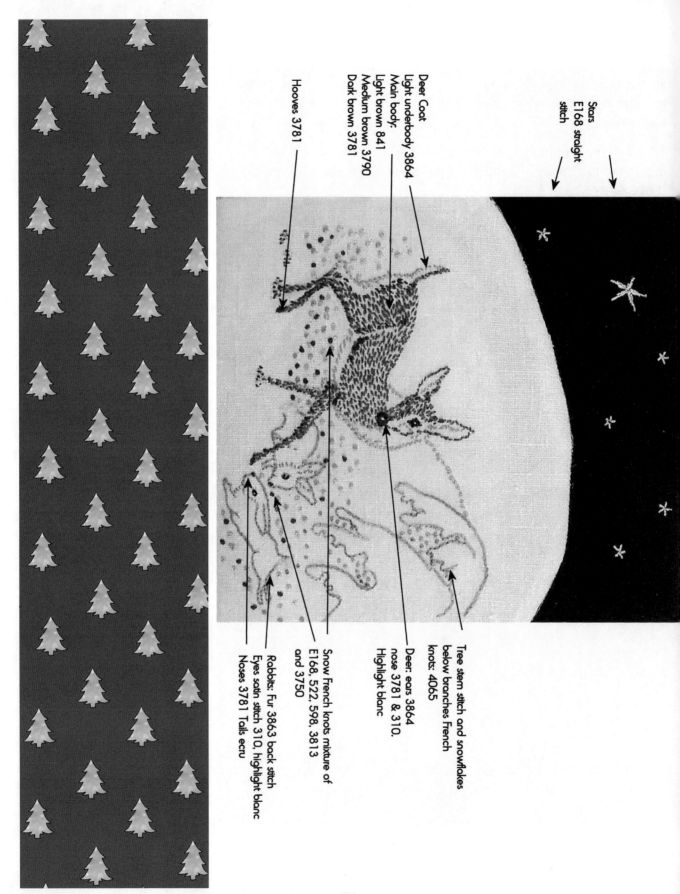

Stars
E168 straight
stitch

Deer Coat
Light underbody 3864
Main body:
Light brown 841
Medium brown 3790
Dark brown 3781

Hooves 3781

Tree stem stitch and snowflakes
below branches French
knots: 4065

Deer: ears 3864
nose 3781 & 310.
Highlight blanc

Snow French knots mixture of
E168, 522, 598, 3813
and 3750

Rabbits: Fur 3863 back stitch
Eyes satin stitch 310, highlight blanc
Noses 3781 Tails ecru

74

"I Saw Three Ships" Table Runner

This is a wonderful pattern for using up all those tiny scraps of fabric - and for turning not very much indeed into a unique Christmas work of art - sure to be treasured and brought out year after year!

Finished size 50" x 18" (approx)

You will need:

- 30 x 5" squares festive fabrics for the patchwork border *(I used a Moda charm pack: Dear Mr Claus by Cosmo Cricket)*
- 32" x 12" cream medium weight fabric for background (quilting weight will not be strong enough to take all the machine embroidery/applique)
- 52" x 20" medium weight fabric for backing
- 32" x 4" strip of dark blue fabric for sea
- Lots of scraps of felt, fabrics and some ric rac braid to create your applique picture.
- Stranded cotton floss in light gold-brown, brown, black, pink and gold
- Bondaweb and temporary fabric adhesive
- Temporary fabric marker pen
- Embroidery/darning foot for your machine
- Black and cream thread for your machine

Applique Panel:

This is huge fun to create. There's nothing particularly difficult about it - simply stick your pieces down and stitch … but there are lots of layers and some of the pieces are quite small, so I would recommend setting aside some clear time to concentrate on one ship at a time to make sure that, for example, you don't suddenly discover you've stuck down an angel's head without first applying the halo behind it!

- Take your cream fabric and fold the two short edges together to find the centre point. Measure 2" up from the bottom edge and mark this point. This will be the position of the centre of the bottom edge of your middle ship (Mary and Jesus).

- Using the templates (they are given at 75% of actual size) at the end of the pattern, trace the ship body and sail onto your bondaweb and fuse to the back of the fabric you have chosen for these shapes. Cut out the shapes but do not remove the Bondaweb at this point. (from now on I will assume you will always trace and fuse the Bondaweb before cutting out your shapes).

- Now cut out and position your shapes for Jesus and Mary - keep checking they fit correctly into the ship by placing your ship sail and body around them as you work

- Note: work from the back forwards - so position your halo first - cutting a little extra so it will underlap the heads, then the heads, with slightly longer necks to underlap the bodies. This avoids any awkward joins or ugly gaps.

- When you're happy with the positioning remove Bondaweb and fuse into place.
- Position your ship body and sail shapes and fuse into place.
- Then the trims and decorations on the ship - be sure to fuse the ends of the ric-rac braid beneath the fabric rectangles at either end of the ship.

- Draw in the lines for the mast and rigging with your temporary fabric marker pen.
- Machine stitch around the edges of your shapes, going around twice (except for figures) and aiming for a scribbled effect.
- Machine stitch the rigging. DO NOT stitch the mast and spar at the front of the ship - you will hand embroider these

- Then hand stitch the mast (using parallel rows of chain stitch and dark brown) and the spar (chain stitch and light golden brown). Stitch the figures' hair. Add rosy cheeks and little black eyes

- Repeat these stages with the other two ships. The ships are positioned 3" apart and there are close up photos of the appliques on the next pages to follow.
- The angel in the first ship is blowing a trumpet - I added some musical notes in black floss to my design.
- When your ship appliques are complete, cut a wavy edge along the top of your dark blue fabric and position to cover the bottom edges of the ships. You might also like to add some green felt shapes as extra waves.
- When happy with your sea, stitch into place. (you could add some fish too, if you wanted!)

Assemble your table runner:

- When your applique is finished press lightly on the reverse

- Take your 5" squares and arrange them around the edge of your applique to decide upon the layout you would like - there will be 7 along the top and bottom of your panel and two and blocks of 8 at each side.

- *Note: all seam allowances are ¼"*

- Join the bottom 7 squares into a strip and using the stitch and flip technique sew them to your applique panel. Position the strip so that just a small amount of sea is showing.

- When you've stitched this strip, then trim away any excess applique fabric to ¼"

- Sew your squares into 2 blocks of 3 x 2 for the sides, then stitch to your applique in the same way, trimming away excess applique fabric.

- Finally add your top 11 squares as a single strip so you've created your patchwork border for your table runner.

- Place your backing fabric and panel right sides together and stitch around the edges, leaving a 6" gap for turning.

- Clip corners and turn right side out. Press, then top stitch around edges ¼" from edge, including over your turning gap.

- Press again - FINISHED!!

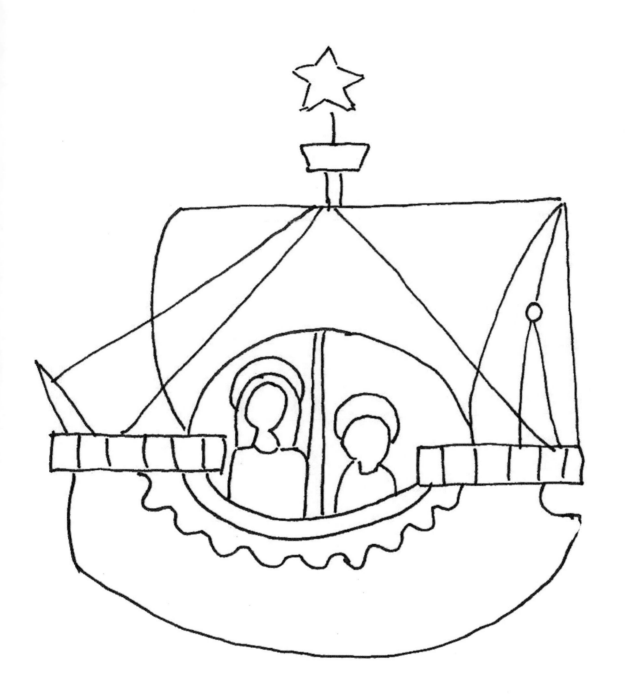

And finally . . .

Two little projects to help you transport all your gifts and purchases at Christmas time. There's a very cheerful reindeer as well as the giraffe I promised you back at the beginning of this book.

I do hope you've enjoyed all my Christmas projects - and if so you might like to visit my website where you'll find projects to enjoy the whole year round.

www.bustleandsew.com

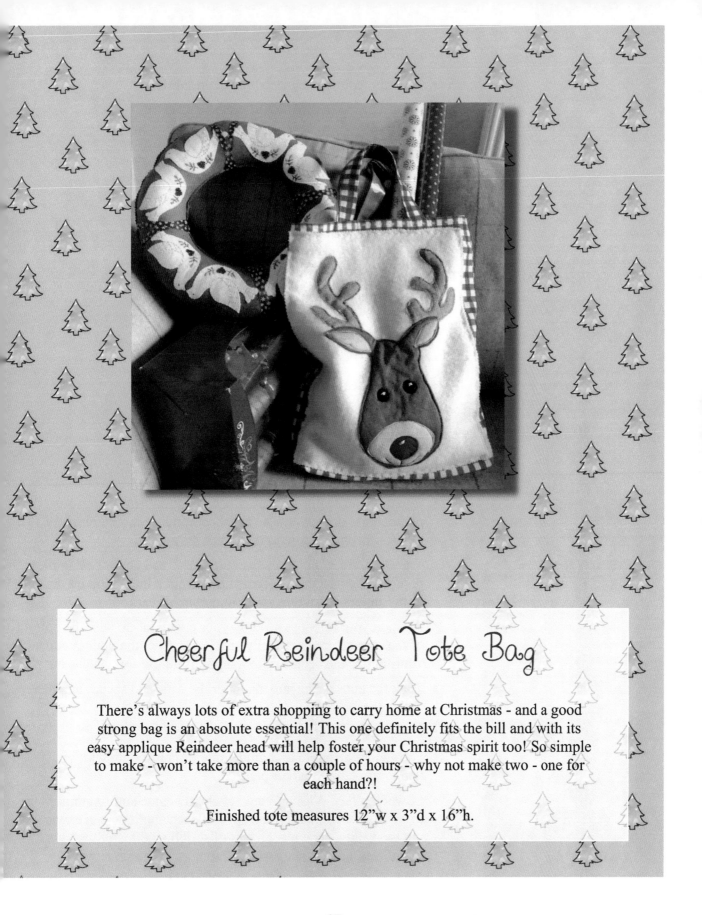

Cheerful Reindeer Tote Bag

There's always lots of extra shopping to carry home at Christmas - and a good strong bag is an absolute essential! This one definitely fits the bill and with its easy applique Reindeer head will help foster your Christmas spirit too! So simple to make - won't take more than a couple of hours - why not make two - one for each hand?!

Finished tote measures 12"w x 3"d x 16"h.

You will need:

- ¾ yard medium weight red gingham fabric
- ¾ yard lining fabric
- 15" x 12" rectangle cream felt
- 9" square brown felt
- 4" square light brown felt
- 8" square tweedy brown fabric
- Scraps of red and black felt
- Black and cream thread for sewing machine needle
- Embroidery foot for machine
- White embroidery floss or perle
- Temporary fabric marker
- Temporary fabric adhesive spray
- Pinking shears (optional)

Note: Seam allowance is ¼"

Create your applique:

- Trim ¼" around the edges of your cream felt with pinking shears (optional, but does look nice).
- Enlarge your template - either use the grid method or use a photocopier or printer. The finished reindeer should measure 13" (approx) from his chin to the top of his antlers.
- Trace individual components onto fabric and cut out using the photo above as a guide. Remember to cut a little extra on the ends of his antlers so that they will underlap his ears.
- Position your reindeer head on your cream fabric with the bottom of the chin centred vertically and ¾" up from the bottom edge of your fabric, and secure with temporary fabric spray adhesive
- Tuck the ends of the antlers under the ears, and secure in place with adhesive.
- Complete the rest of the head in the same way.
- Following the photo as a guide, mark in his mouth with your temporary fabric marker pen.
- Lower the feed dogs on your sewing machine and fit embroidery foot. Then stitch around the edge of each applique piece twice, not too neatly - you want a sort of scribbled effect. Stitch his mouth and lines to suggest a round nose in the same way.

- With your white floss or perle thread, stitch highlights for his eyes and a shiny bit on his nose.
- Remove the temporary marker lines.
- Your reindeer is now finished.

Make your Tote Bag:

- From your red gingham fabric cut two rectangles, each measuring 12 ½" x 18" and two strips, each measuring 2" x 14".
- Repeat with your lining fabric .
- Take one piece of red gingham fabric and position your applique panel centrally with the top edge 1" down from the top edge of the red gingham.
- Secure with spray adhesive, or pin/baste then machine stitch into place around the edges with cream thread in your needle. I used a decorativestitch to add a little extra textural interest, but this is not essential.
- Place your two pieces of red gingham together with right sides facing and join around 3 edges, leaving the top edge open.
- Make the box shape for the bottom of the bag by centering one of the side seams so it lines up with the bottom seam. Pinch the seams together and lay the bag on your work surface. Use pins to hold the seams together.
- Use a ruler and measure up 1 1/2" from the point of the fabric and draw a line (dotted line on diagram). The line should measure 3" long with 1 1/2" of fabric on either side of the seam.
- Repeat this for the other side of the tote bag.
- To complete the box bottom of the tote bag, sew along each line you drew. Lock stitch (sew back and forth) when you start and when you finish sewing.
- Trim the threads and then cut off the points, leaving about 1/2" fabric.
- Repeat with the lining, but leave a gap of 4" at the base of the lining for turning at the end.
- To make handles, take your four small strips (2 outer fabric and 2 lining fabric) and turn over ¼" down the long sides.
- Place the strips wrong sides together and machine along each long edge less than ¼" from the edge, hiding the raw edges.
- Turn the lining right side out and place inside bag outer, aligning top edges and matching side seams.
- Lay the tote bag on its side.

- At the top edge of the tote bag, measure 4" from each seam. Mark with a straight pin.
- Line up the outside edge of one end of a handle with one of the straight pins. Hold the end of the handle so it lines up with the top edge of the tote bag and pin in place. (the handle will be down inside the bag, between the lining and the outer)
- Pin the other end of the handle in place next to the other straight pin using this same method. Make sure that you match the lining side of the handle to the bag lining.
- Pin or tack all around the top edge of the bag then machine stitch together.
- Remove ALL pins (if you leave them in you'll be unable to remove them easily once you've turned the bag)
- Turn the bag right side out through the gap you left in the lining. .Machine stitch the gap closed.
- Push lining down inside bag and press all around top edge.
- Machine stitch around top edge ¼ " from the edge or less for a nice neat finish that will help the lining stay in place.
- Press seams.
- FINISHED!!

Giraffe Bottle Bag

Who says Christmas is just for robins and reindeer? This little giraffe is happy to help out – very carefully holding his Christmas candle - a perfect way to present your Christmas gift bottle – and lovely to keep as well.

This bag is the perfect size for a standard bottle of wine – but you can resize it to fit whatever size you want…

You will need:

- 1   piece of medium-weight canvas measuring 13 ½" tall x 17" wide
- 1   piece of medium-weight canvas cut into a 5" diameter circle
- 17" length ric-rac braid
- 16" x 1" wide cream cotton twill tape
- 10 x 4" piece fawn coloured felt
- 4" square brown felt
- Scraps of red and green felt for candle and holly leaves
- Embroidery floss in yellow, orange, black and red
- Bondaweb or fabric adhesive
- Pinking shears
- Erasable fabric marker
- Cream, red and brown machine thread

Create your applique:

- Fold your large piece of canvas in half vertically to find the centre and measure 2 ½" up from the bottom.

- Cut your giraffe shape in fawn felt and secure to the base canvas with Bondaweb or adhesive (whichever you prefer), positioning it on your centre fold and 2 ½" up from the bottom.

- Mark in the lines for his legs using your erasable fabric marker pen

- With brown thread in your machine needle and a paler coloured thread in the bobbin (if you use brown in both then your stitching will appear too hard), stitch twice around the giraffe's body. Stitch in his legs, following the lines you marked with your fabric pen. Make zig-zag shapes for his tail end, hooves and mane.

- Cut out his patches in brown felt and apply to his body with fabric adhesive or Bondaweb as preferred. Machine stitch around the edges.

- Cut out the holly leaves in green felt and machine stitch into place. Stitch a centre vein down the middle of each leaf and across his neck between the leaves.

- Cut out the candle in red felt and machine stitch in place.

- Embroider 3 red holly berries in red floss, the giraffe's eye in black and the candle flame in orange and yellow.

ACTUAL SIZE

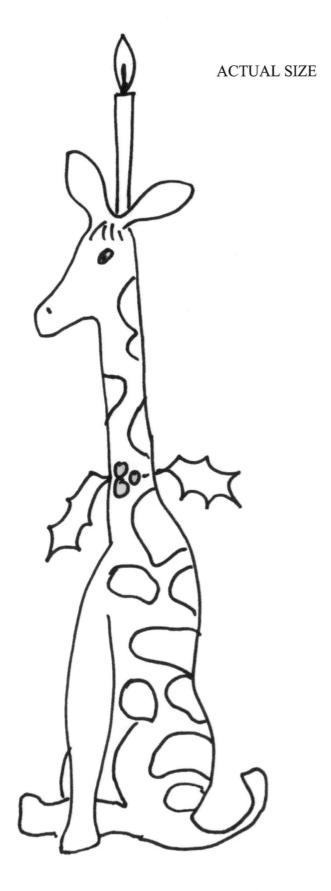

Make your gift bag:

- With red thread in your machine needle, Stitch ric-rac braid to top of main piece, 2" down from top edge.

- Fold your canvas right sides together and machine down the two shorter edges of the canvas with a ½" seam allowance using cream thread.

- Trim the seam with pinking shears to prevent excess fraying (as this is a gift bag I have not lined it, but it would be easy to include a lining if you wished).

- Sew the base to the main body of the bag and trim the seam with pinking shears.

- Turn right side out.

- Trim top edge with pinking shears, turn 1 ½" to the inside and machine ¾" down from the top edge.

- Trim ends of twill tape with pinking shears and machine stitch to the inside of the bag, equidistant from the back seam and the centre front. Go over your stitching several times for strength.

- Change to red thread in your machine needle and stitch the ric-rac braid to the top over your machine stitching.

- Press back seam lightly if necessary. Insert bottle and enjoy!!

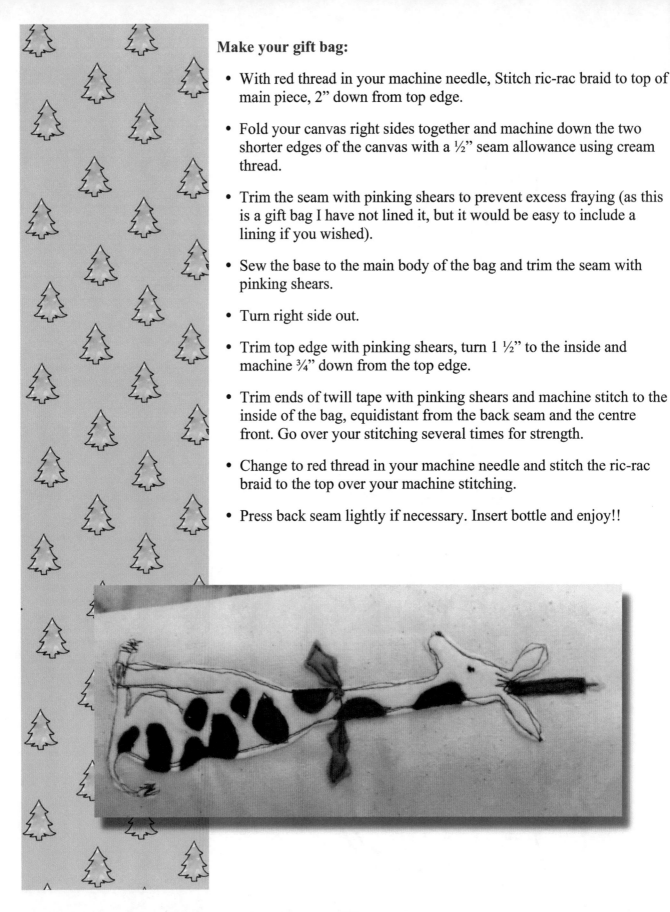

Bustle and Sew Magazine

Before I go off to put my mince pies in the oven (!) , I just wanted to tell you a little bit about my Bustle & Sew Magazine - positively the nicest and best way to build your collection of Bustle & Sew patterns.

Try the Bustle & Sew Magazine for just $1 and receive the Stitcher's Companion absolutely free!

The Bustle & Sew magazine is a monthly e-magazine delivered direct to your email in-box on the last Thursday of each month ready to read in 2 formats … firstly on Issuu.com – which lets you read the magazine on your computer screen and also as a normal pdf file – which is quick and easy to download and print.

So if you're like me and have a stash of irresistible fabrics, just waiting for you to find the perfect project to show them off in all their glory, I'm sure you'll enjoy my magazine.

You can try it for an initial payment of just $1 - and receive my full-length e-book "The Stitcher's Companion" absolutely free. And what's more - this is a genuine no-risk offer. If for any reason, or no reason at all, you decide not to continue with your subscription, then all you need to do is drop me an email to cancel. That's it - no penalties and no tie-in period.

And it's great value too - every month you'll discover five or six original Bustle & Sew designs, for all levels of stitchers, not all of which will be made available later for individual purchase.

Techniques include…

- Hand and freestyle machine embroidery

- Quilting

- Applique

- Softies

- Bags

And many other projects for your home and family.

The magazine also offers vintage patterns, projects from guest designers, features and articles about all the topics as well as extra information to help you with your own projects.

You can learn more about the magazine and subscribe on the Bustle & Sew website

www.bustleandsew.com

5792702R00055

Printed in Great Britain
by Amazon.co.uk, Ltd.,
Marston Gate.